MW01639948

# Pictures 'n Poems 1,2,3

by **Marybeth Fox Soutar**
illustrations by **Lindsey Fu**

Dedicated to my mother, who taught me how to put myself in someone else's shoes.

Copyright
Marybeth Fox Soutar

Pictures 'n Poems 1,2,3
© 2014 Marybeth Fox Soutar

Self publishing

www.pictures-n-poems.com

Nifty Newmonics, LLC
P.O. Box 391
Morris Plains, NJ 07950

**All rights reserved.**

---

This book contains material protected under International and Federal Copyright Laws and Treaties. Any unauthorized reprint or use of this material is prohibited. No part of this book may be reproduced or transmitted in any form or by any means, electronic or mechanical, including photocopying, recording, or by any information storage and retrieval system without express written permission from the author/publisher. The author has made every effort to trace the ownership of all copyrighted material and to secure the necessary permissions to reprint these selections. In the event of any question arising as to the use of any material, the author, while expressing regret for any inadvertent error, will be happy to make any necessary corrections.

---

ISBN 978-0-9863363-0-0

Pictures and poems for Math are quite rare.
We often see numbers on pages and stare.
But, numbers stand tall and have stories to tell
So, *Pictures 'n Poems* expresses that well!

These pictures hide numbers in dark pirate ships,
In big trucks and chute-packs for skydiving trips!
The rhymes describe donuts and burgers and fries,
A cool magic wand and a spaceman who flies!

We'll see them and read them and cuddle and count.
We'll sing and dress up and soon learn the amount!
Creative ideas make the Math come alive,
So kids everywhere can numerically thrive!
Now S.T.E.M. is the future and leadership path
(That's Science, Technology, Engineering and Math!).

# Don't count delicious donuts.

There once was a sweet **zero** sign.
A treat and a number - that's fine!
You munch and you share,
So nothing's left there!
Don't count when you see *donut* sign.

# O is for superhero!

What's the way to make a **zero**?
Zoom around, you superhero!

# Count one dollar.

There once was a wealthy **one** sign.
A buck and a number - that's fine!
A single bill buys
A burger or fries.
Count **one** for the *dollar bill* sign!

1 is for wand!
What's the way to make a **one**?
Trace the wand for magic fun!

# Count two twins.

There once was a double **two** sign.
Two babes and a number - that's fine!
On hands and on knees,
Twins scoot by with ease!
Count **two** when you see the *twins* sign.

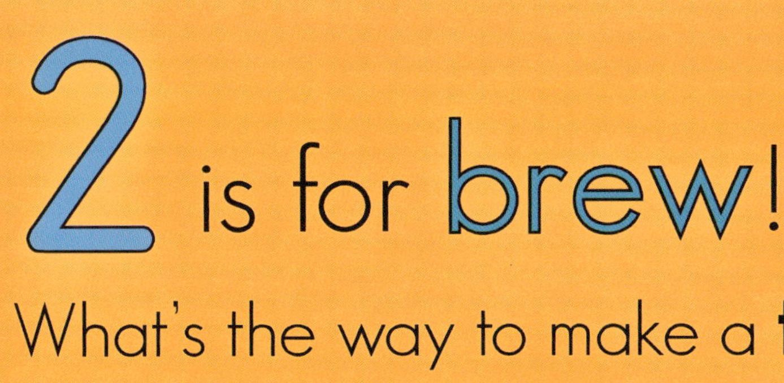

# 2 is for brew!

What's the way to make a **two**?
Sketch a mug of nice, hot brew!

# Count three wheels.

There once was a triple **three** sign.
Three wheels and a number – that's fine!
The front wheel is wide.
The back wheels just glide.
Count **three** for the *tricycle* sign.

# 3 is for tree!

What's the way to make a **three**?
See balloons stuck in a tree!

# Count **four** squares.

There once was a friendly **four** sign.
Four-square and a number – that's fine!
You're Ace and you serve;
You make the ball curve!
Count **four** when you see *Four-square* sign.

# 4 is for fork!

What's the way to make a **four**?
Pound your fork if you want more!

# Count five fingers.

There once was a handy **five** sign.
A hand and a number – that's fine!
She's raising her hand.
Five fingers expand!
Count **five** when you see *fingers* sign.

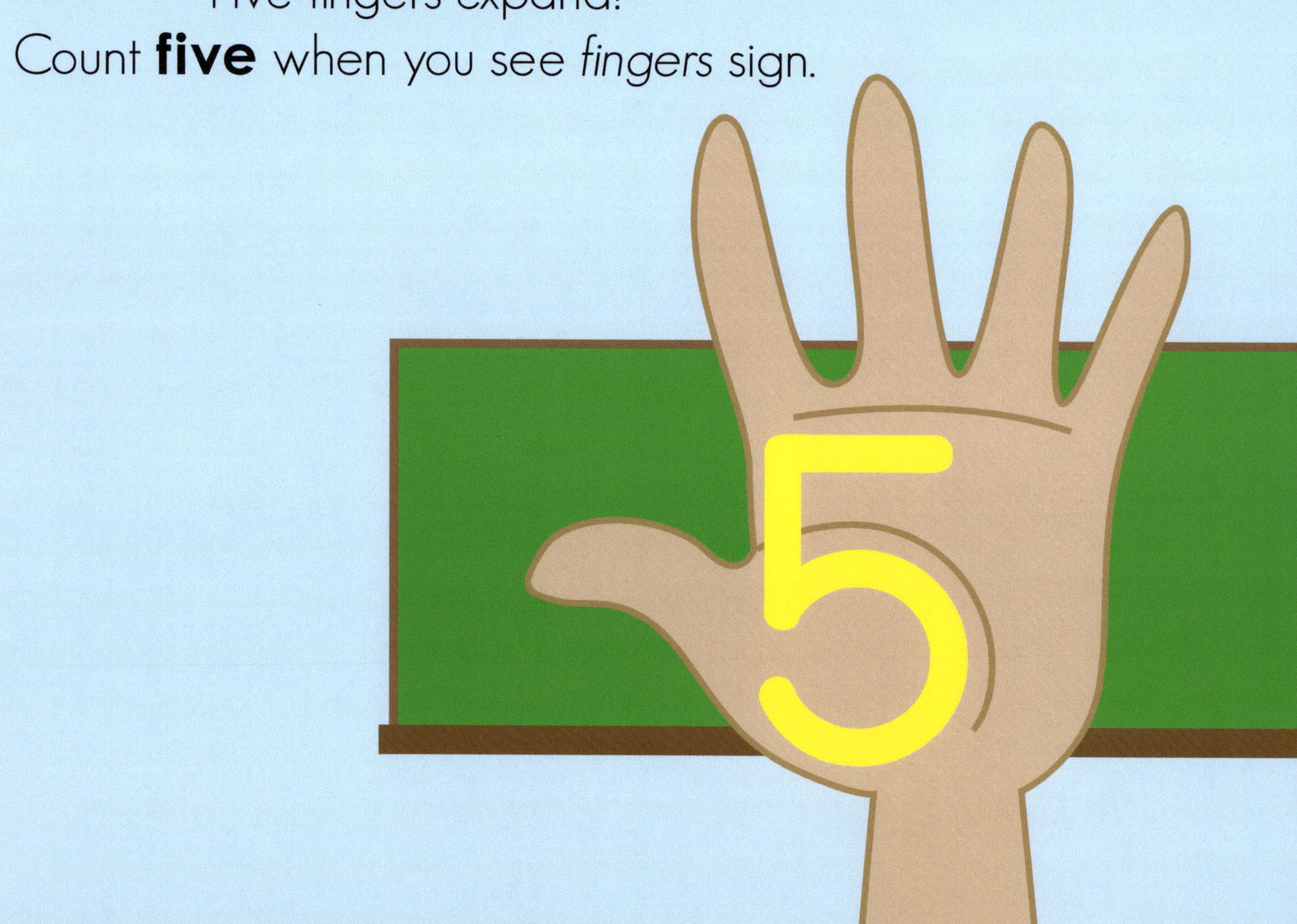

# 5 is for drive!

What's the way to make a **five**?
Draw his seat, then arms to drive!

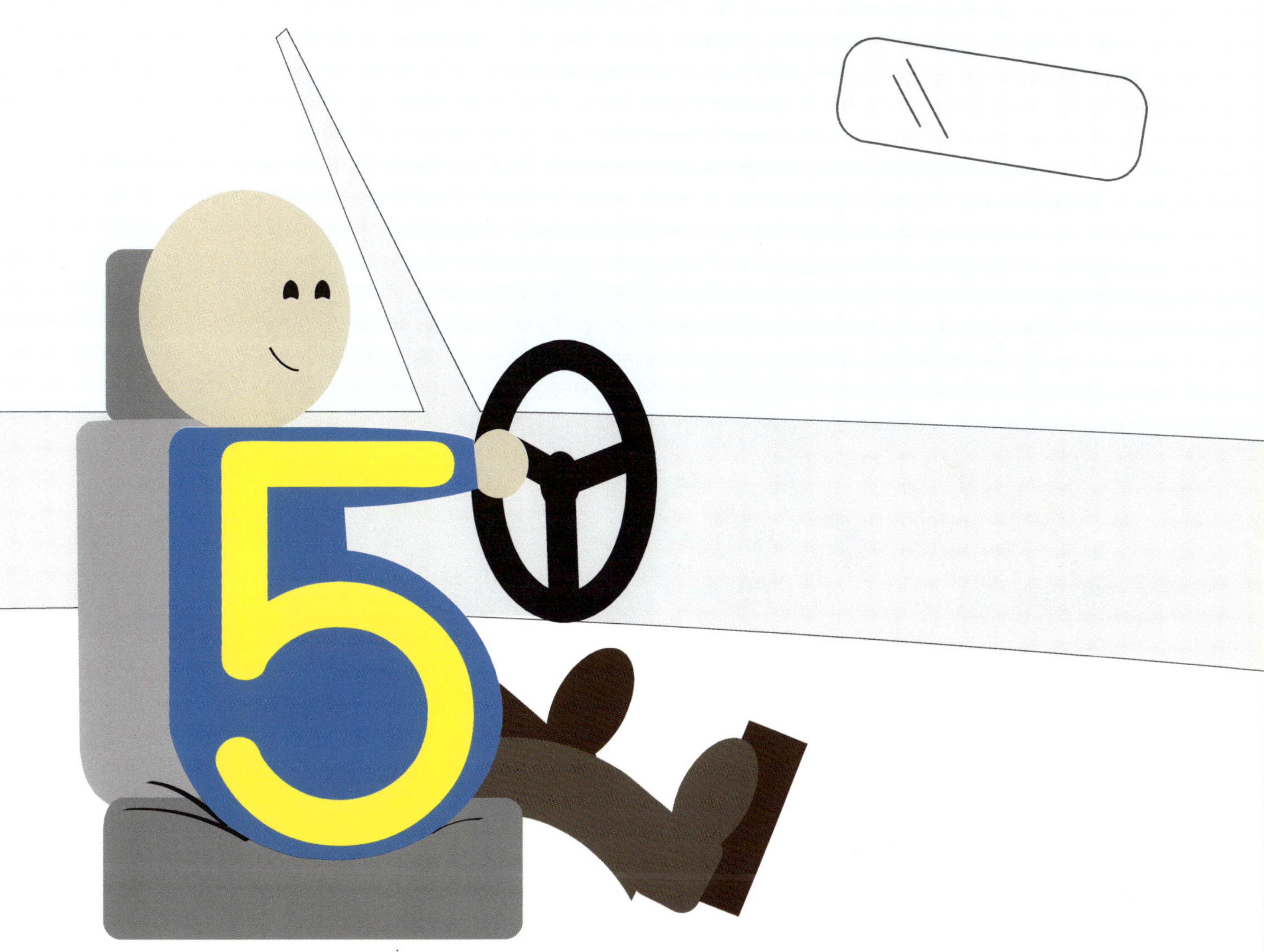

# Count six strings.

There once was a singing **six** sign.
Six strings and a number - that's fine!
Guitars wired tight-
The music sounds right!
Count **six** when you see *six-string* sign.

# 6 is for witches' mix!

What's the way to make a **six**?
Witches swirl the bubbling mix!

# Count seven red stripes.

There once was a steep **seven** sign.
A flag and a number – that's fine!
Count seven stripes red.
It flies overhead!
Count **seven** for *stars and stripes* sign.

# 7 is for heaven!

What's the way to make a **seven**?
Cross the sky and down from heaven!

# Count eight hours.

There once was a noisy **eight** sign.
A clock and a number entwine!
Eight hours of sleep:
Good habit to keep!
Count **eight** when you see the *clock* sign.

# 8 is for plates!

What's the way to make an **eight**?
Draw two plates that line up straight!

# Count nine fielders.

There once was a baseball **nine** sign,
Nine guys and a number - that's fine!
Nine fielders below -
It starts with a throw.
Count **nine** for the *baseball field* sign.

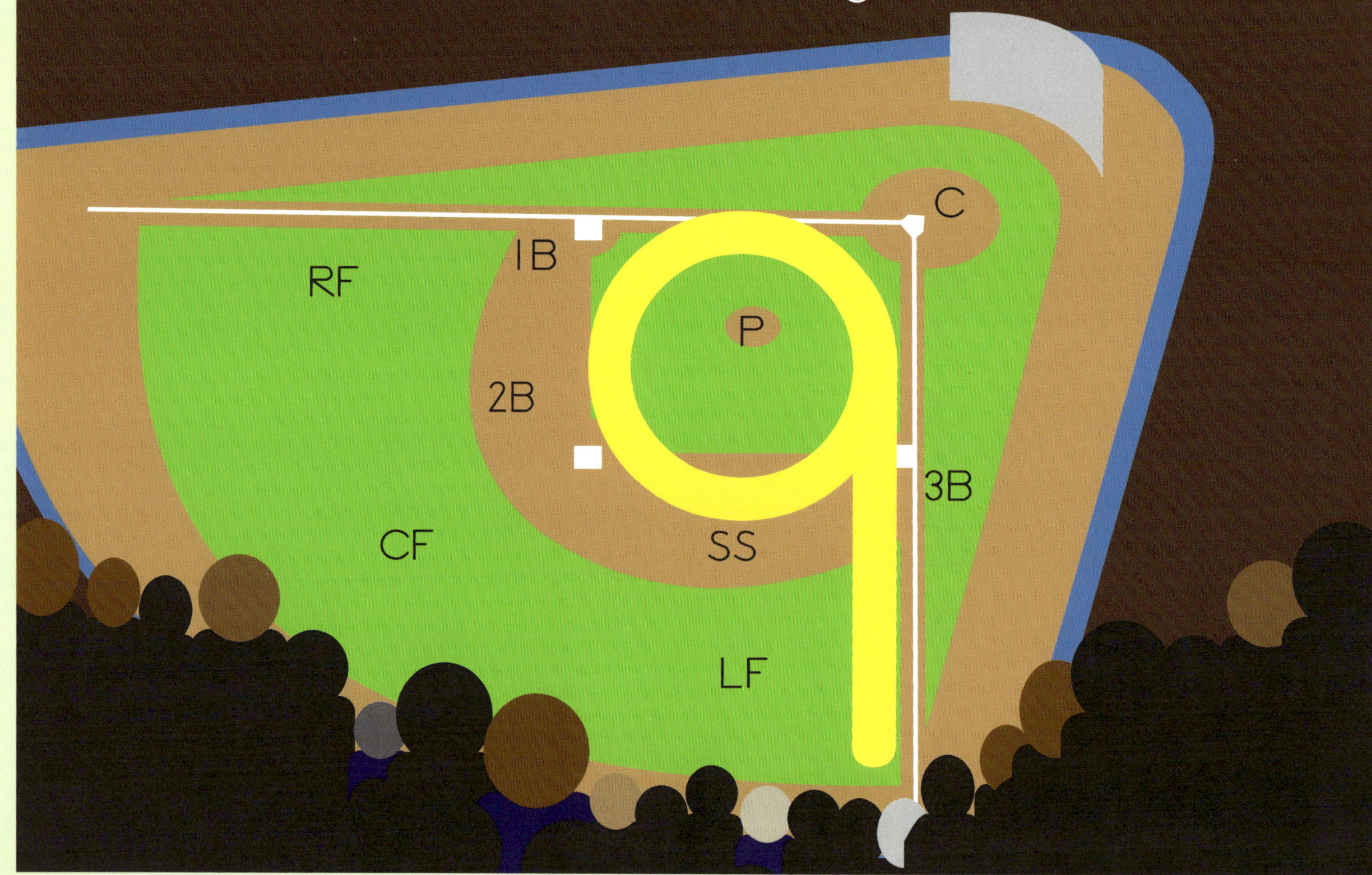

# 9 is for **mountain climb**!

What's the way to make a **nine**?
Strap your pack along your spine!

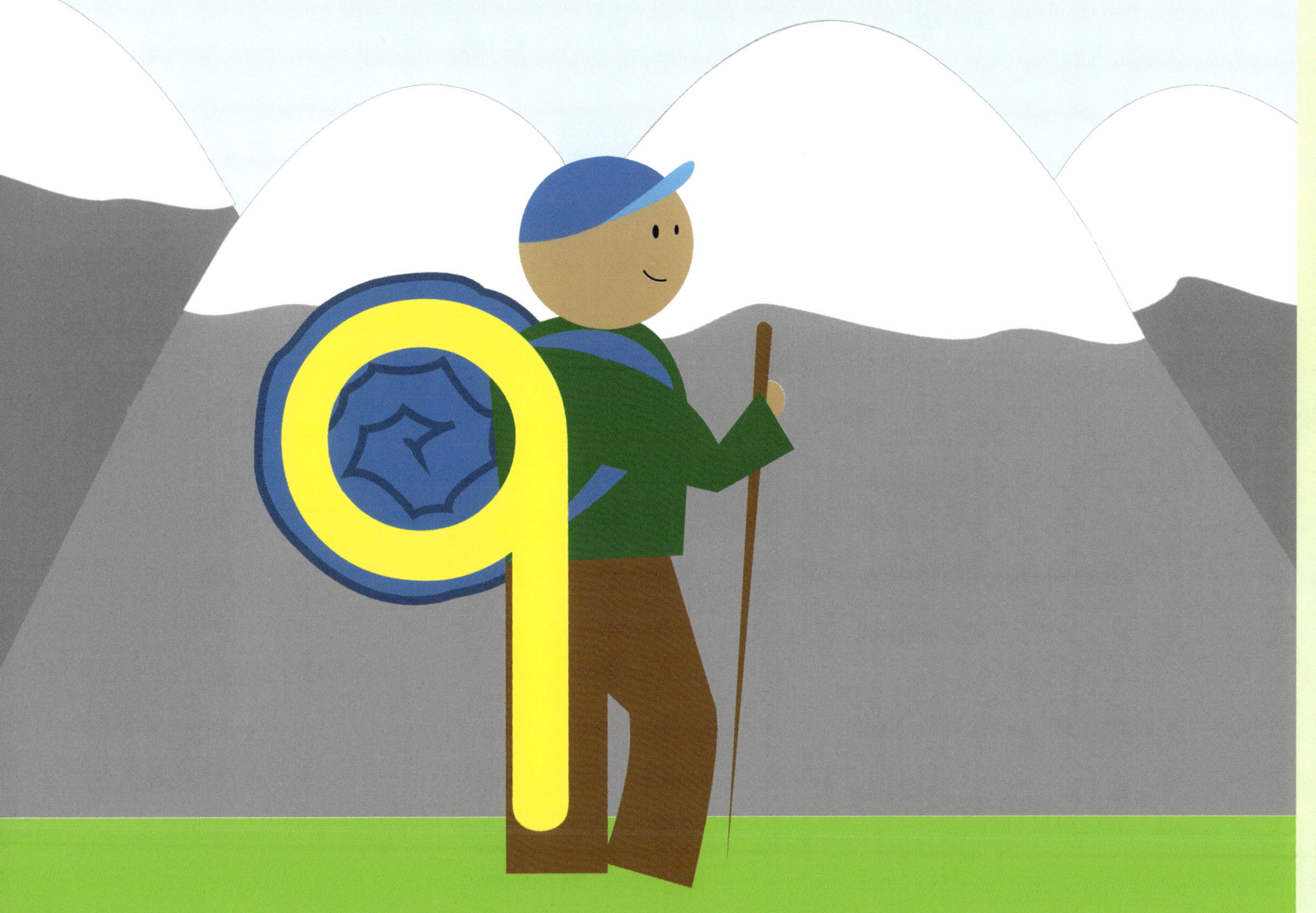

# Count ten burgers.

There once was a little **ten** sign.
Ten grilled and a number - that's fine!
Ten burgers per pack
Cook fast on the rack.
Count **ten** for the *grilled burger* sign.

# 10 is for lens!

What's the way to make your **tens**?
Draw a pirate and her lens!

*Now, you know the shape and sign*
*For every number on a line.*
*So, trace them with your finger now.*
*The rhymes and arrows tell you how.*
*The starting arrow's high and black.* ▼
*The next one takes a light gray track.* ▽
*Writing numbers is the way*
*To show you're clever every day!*

# 1 is for wand!

What's the way to make a **one**?
Trace the wand for magic fun!

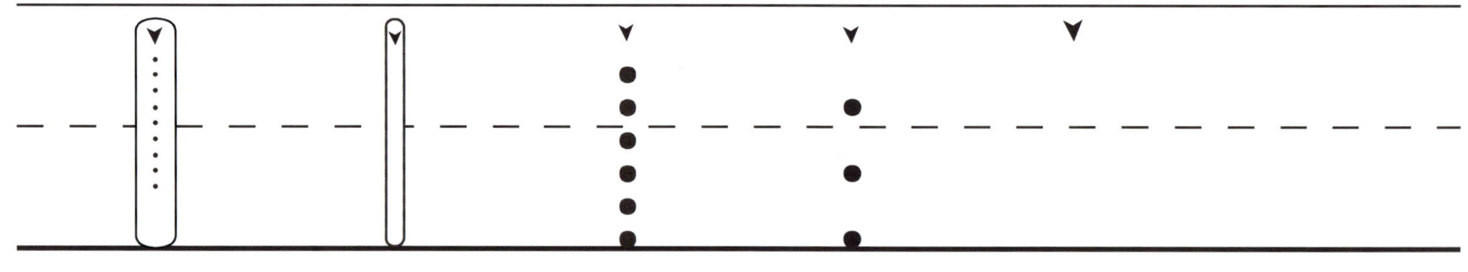

# 0 is for superhero!

What's the way to make a **zero**?
Zoom around, you superhero!

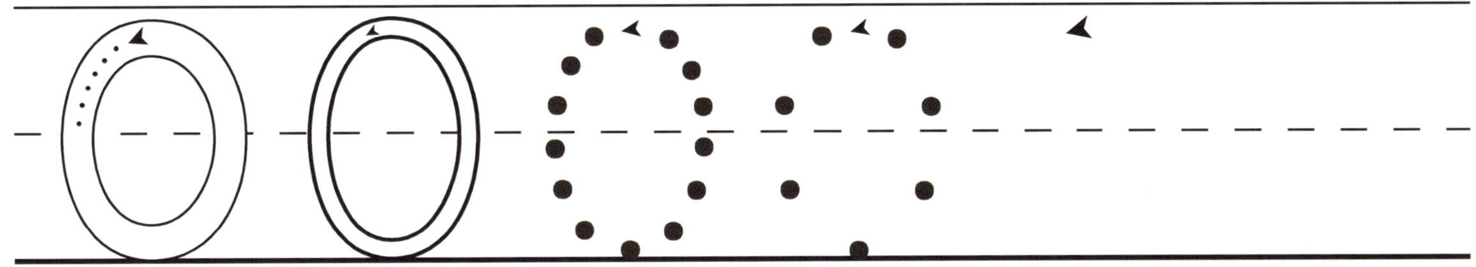

# 2 is for brew!

What's the way to make a **two**?
Sketch a mug with nice, hot brew!

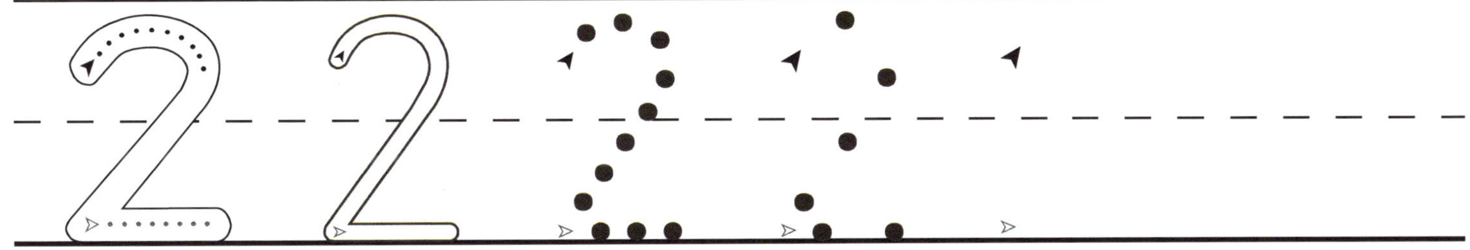

# 3 is for tree!

What's the way to make a **three**?
See balloons stuck in a tree!

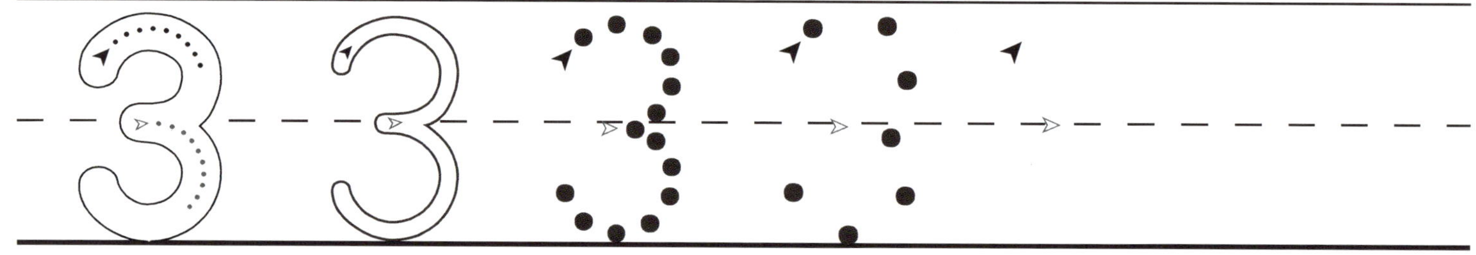

# 5 is for drive!

What's the way to make a **five**?
Draw his seat, then arms to drive!

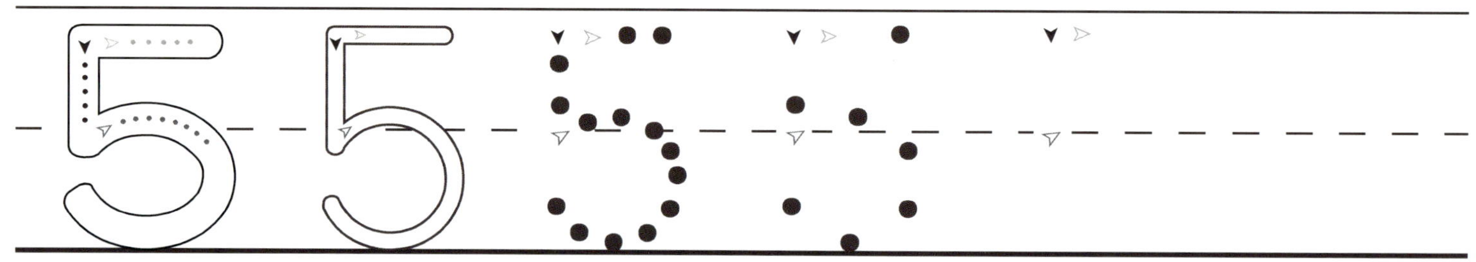

# 4 is for fork!

What's the way to make a **four**?
Pound your fork if you want more!

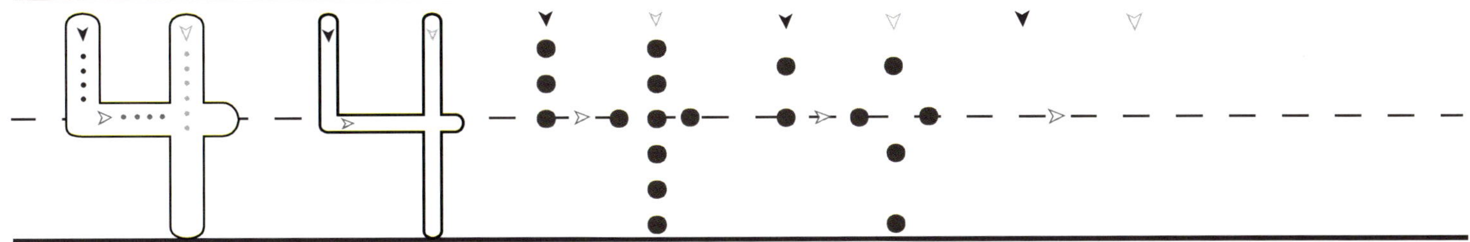

# 6 is for witches' mix!

What's the way to make a **six**?
Witches swirl the bubbling mix!

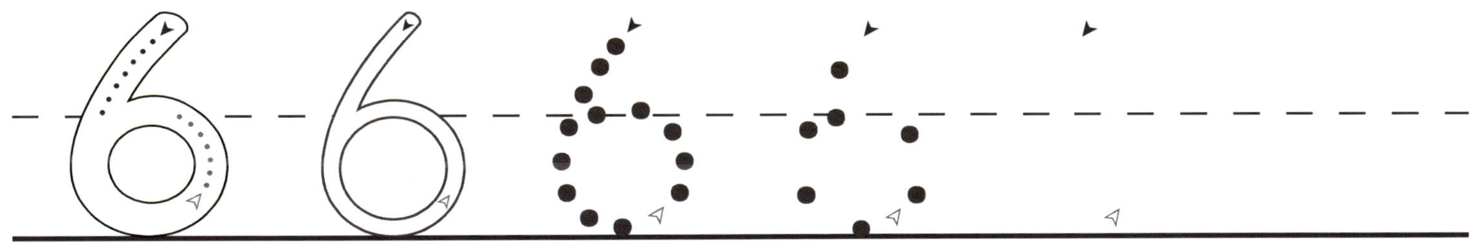

# 7 is for heaven!

What's the way to make a **seven**?
Cross the sky and down from heaven!

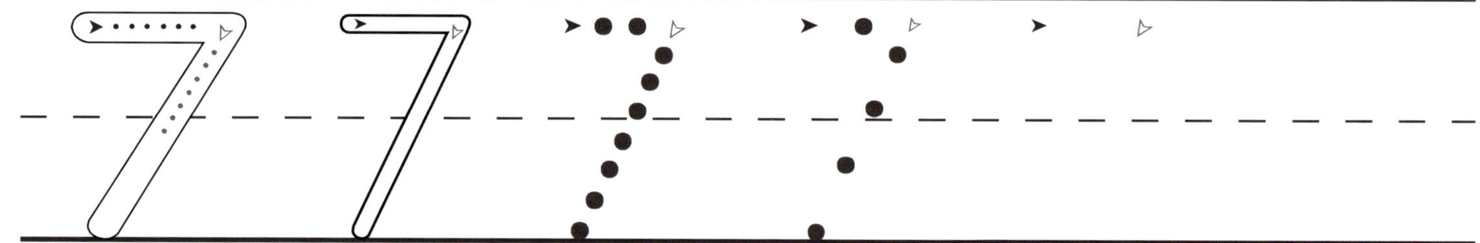

# 9 is for mountain climb!

What's the way to make a **nine**?
Strap your pack along your spine!

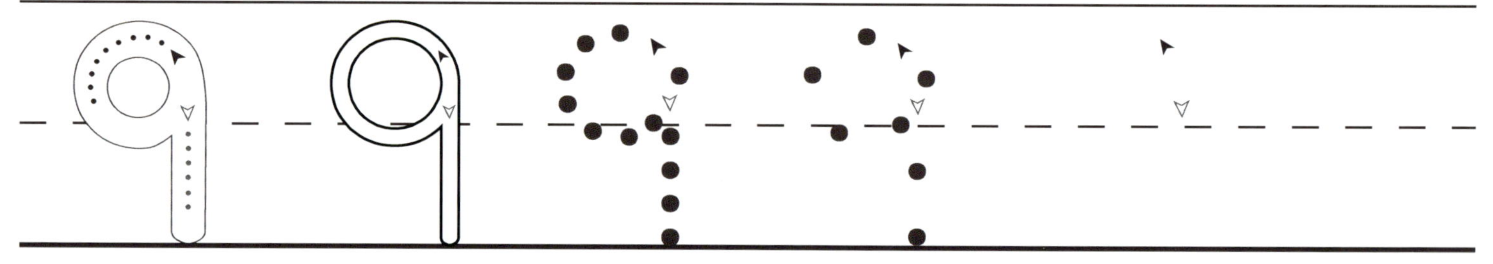

# 8 is for plates!

What's the way to make an **eight**?
Draw two plates that line up straight!

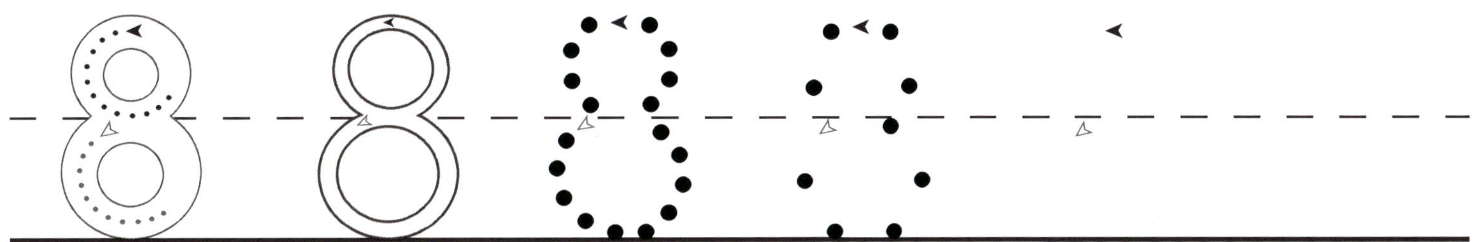

# 10 is for lens!

What's the way to make a **ten**?
Draw a pirate and her lens!

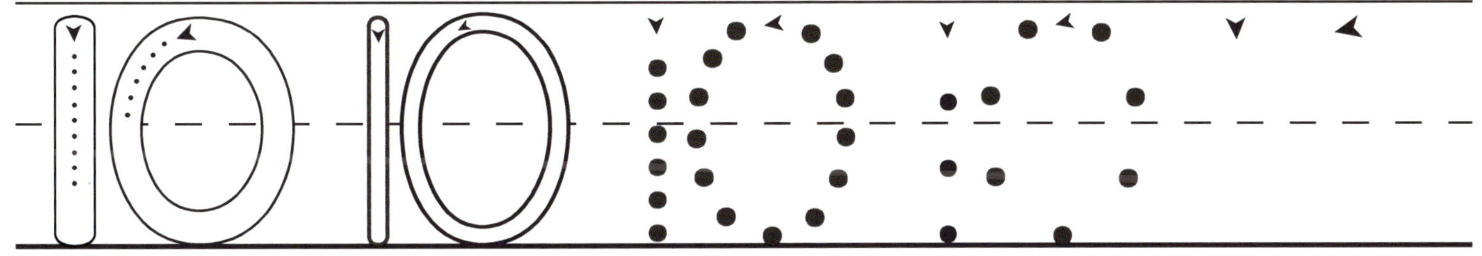

Let's practice counting!

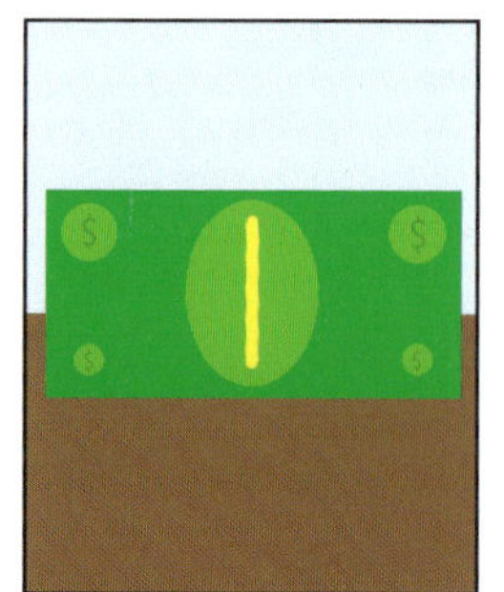

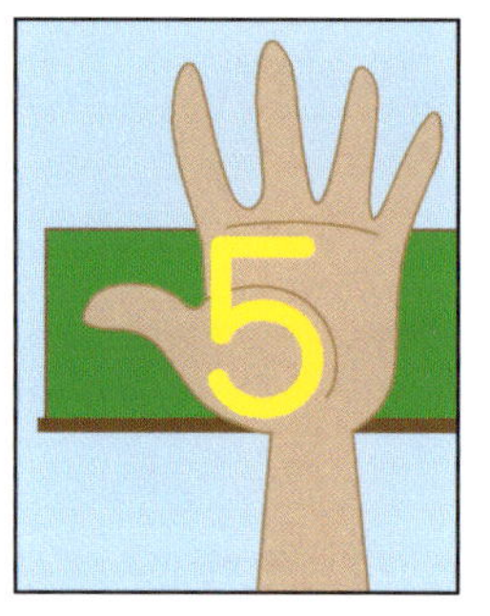

One more time...

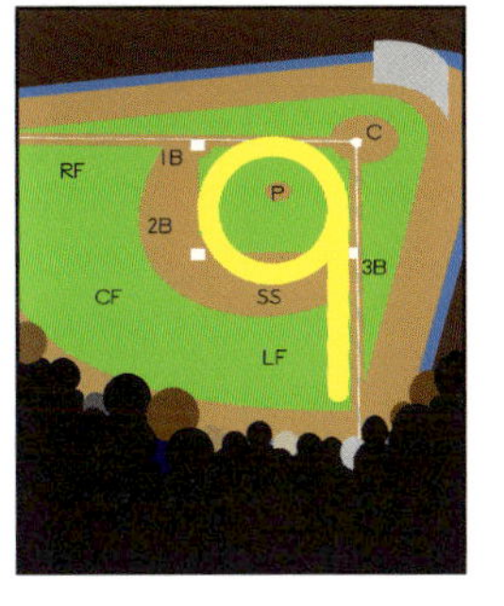
C
RF
1B
P
2B
3B
CF
SS
LF

CPSIA information can be obtained at www.ICGtesting.com
Printed in the USA
BVIW12n0254210815
413505BV00001BA/1